DC COMICS™

BATMAN™ ORIGAMI

AMAZING FOLDING PROJECTS FEATURING THE DARK KNIGHT

Published by Capstone Press in 2015
A Capstone Imprint
1710 Roe Crest Drive
North Mankato, Minnesota 56003
www.capstonepub.com

STAR35424

Library of Congress Cataloging-in-Publication Data
Montroll, John, author.
  Batman origami : amazing folding projects featuring the dark
knight / by John Montroll ; Batman created by Bob Kane.
      pages cm.—(DC super heroes. DC origami)
  Summary: "Provides instructions and diagrams for folding
origami models of characters, objects, and symbols related to
Batman"—Provided by publisher.
  Audience: Age 8-12.
  Audience: Grades 4-6.
  Includes bibliographical references.
  ISBN 978-1-4914-1786-7 (library binding)
  ISBN 978-1-4914-7593-5 (eBook PDF)
1. Origami—Juvenile literature. 2. Batman (Fictitious
character)—Juvenile literature. 3. Superheroes in art—Juvenile
literature. 4. Supervillains in art—Juvenile literature. 5.
Handicraft—Juvenile literature. I. Kane, Bob, creator. II. Title.
  TT872.5.M644 2015
  736'.982—dc23   2015003761

Editorial Credits

Editor and Model Folder: Christopher Harbo
Designer: Lori Bye
Art Directors: Bob Lentz and Nathan Gassman
Contributing Writers: Donald Lemke and Michael Dahl
Folding Paper Illustrator: Min Sung Ku
Production Specialist: Kathy McColley

Photo Credits

Capstone Studio/Karon Dubke, all photos

Printed in the United States of America in North Mankato, MN.
052016 009763R

TABLE OF CONTENTS

Secret Identities

Super heroes may have a wide variety of powers and abilities, but they all have one very important thing in common: a secret identity. For Bruce Wayne, his public life as your average billionaire is just a cover for his secret life on the dark streets of Gotham City. When danger strikes, he transforms. Donning a cape and cowl, he becomes Batman. As the Caped Crusader, he fights for truth and justice to save his city from some of the world's most dangerous super-villains.

Believe it or not, paper has a secret identity too. Through origami, the Japanese art of paper folding, paper gains the power to transform. With a series of folds it morphs from flat and ordinary into something extraordinary. This book contains instructions for 11 amazing paper transformations. From a single square, you will create dynamic models of vehicles, weapons, symbols, and super heroes related to the Dark Knight. From bat-symbols and Batarangs to Batman and Robin, every model will reveal the secret identity hidden in a sheet of paper.

Even if you are a first-time folder, this collection is designed to help you succeed. The folding diagrams are drawn in the internationally approved Randlett-Yoshizawa style. This style is easy to follow once you learn the basic folds outlined in the pages to come. The models are also ranked and organized for their level of difficulty: one star for simple, two stars for intermediate, and three stars for complex. By working through the collection from simplest to most complex, you'll build on your folding skills.

Remember, Bruce Wayne didn't become Batman in one day. He trained his body and mind for years to become the World's Greatest Detective. With patience, practice, and a few bold folds, you can become an origami super hero!

5

Symbols

Lines

— — — — — — — — —   Valley fold, fold in front.

— · · — · · — · · — · · — · · —   Mountain fold, fold behind.

———————————————   Crease line.

·   X-ray or guide line.

Arrows

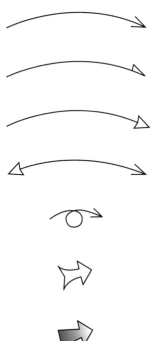

Fold in this direction.

Fold behind.

Unfold.

Fold and unfold.

Turn over.

Sink or three dimensional folding.

 Place your finger between these layers.

BASIC FOLDS

PLEAT FOLD

Fold back and forth. Each pleat is composed of one valley and mountain fold. Here are two examples.

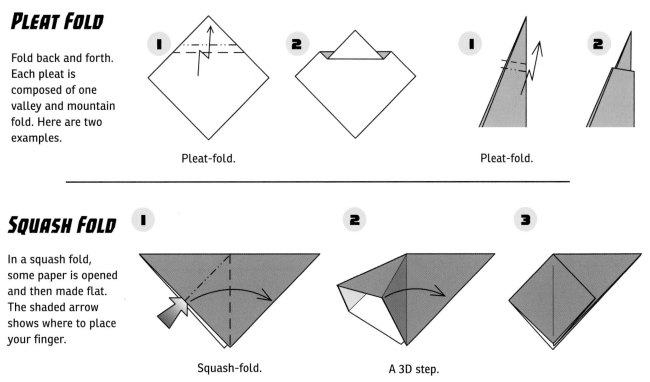

Pleat-fold.

Pleat-fold.

SQUASH FOLD

In a squash fold, some paper is opened and then made flat. The shaded arrow shows where to place your finger.

Squash-fold.

A 3D step.

INSIDE REVERSE FOLD

In an inside reverse fold, some paper is folded between layers. The inside reverse fold is generally referred to as a reverse fold. Here are two examples.

Reverse-fold.

Reverse-fold.

OUTSIDE REVERSE FOLD

Much of the paper must be unfolded to wrap around, in order to make an outside reverse fold.

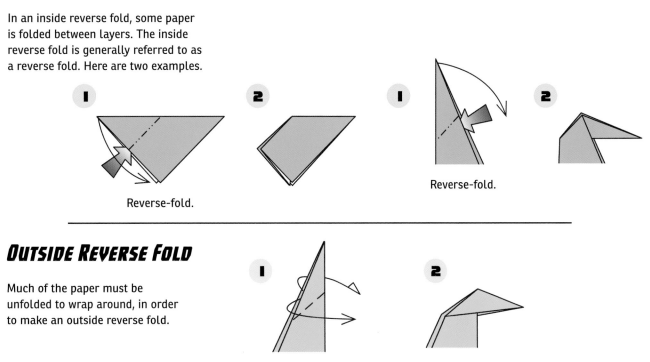

Outside-reverse-fold.

Crimp Fold

A crimp fold is a combination
of two reverse folds. Open
the model slightly to form the
crimp evenly on each side.
Here are two examples.

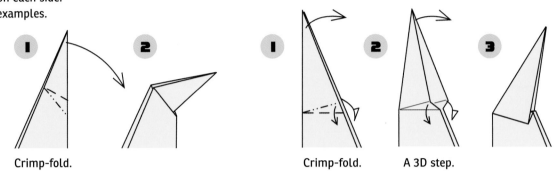

Crimp-fold.   Crimp-fold.   A 3D step.

Rabbit Ear

To fold a rabbit ear, one
corner is folded in half
and laid down to a side.

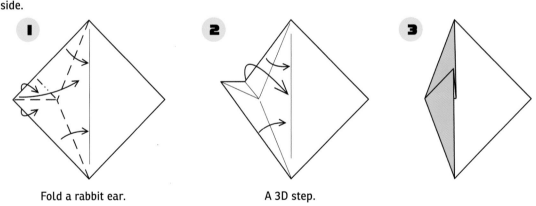

Fold a rabbit ear.   A 3D step.

Spread Squash Fold

A cross between a squash fold and
sink fold, some paper in the center
is spread apart and then made flat.

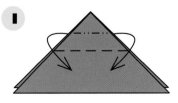
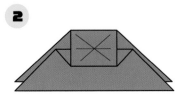

Spread-squash-fold.

THE RIDDLER'S CANE

Even as a little boy, Edward Nygma loved riddles and puzzles. When he grew up, Nygma turned his passion into a career. He became a video game designer and soon invented a popular game called *Riddle of the Minotaur*. The game sold millions of copies, but Nygma didn't receive a dime from the manufacturer. To get his revenge, Nygma became the Riddler, a cryptic criminal who leaves clues about his crimes. The super-villain carries a cane shaped like a question mark. This weapon can deliver a shocking blast—the Riddler's answer to his toughest problems.

LEVEL: ★★☆

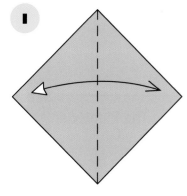

1 Fold and unfold.

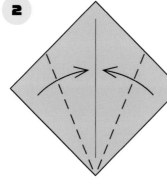

2 Fold to the center.

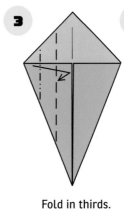

3 Fold in thirds.

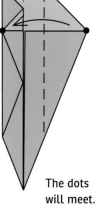

4 The dots will meet.

9

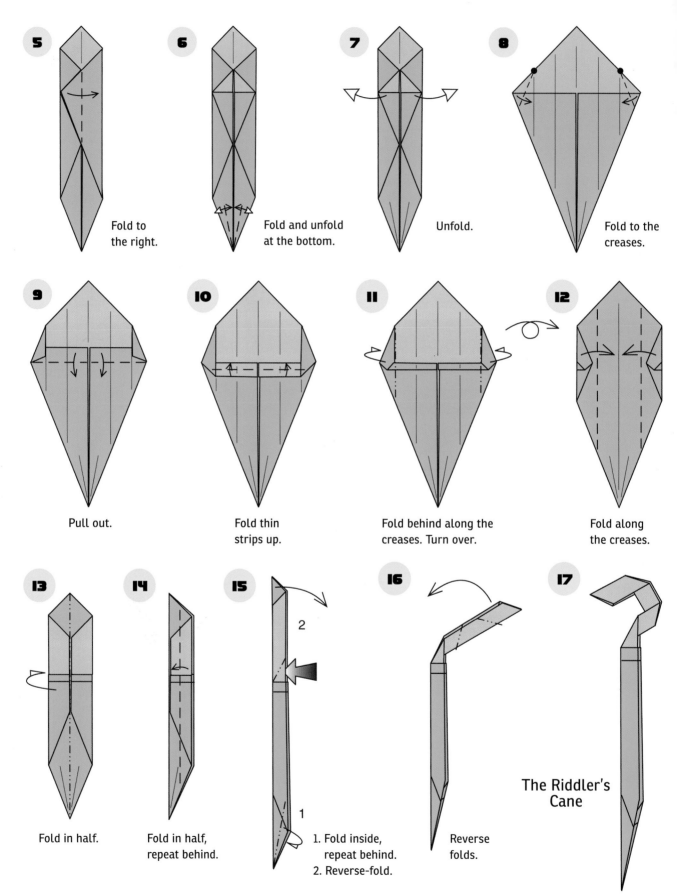

5 Fold to the right.

6 Fold and unfold at the bottom.

7 Unfold.

8 Fold to the creases.

9 Pull out.

10 Fold thin strips up.

11 Fold behind along the creases. Turn over.

12 Fold along the creases.

13 Fold in half.

14 Fold in half, repeat behind.

15
2
1
1. Fold inside, repeat behind.
2. Reverse-fold.

16 Reverse folds.

17

The Riddler's Cane

MAD HATTER'S TOP HAT

Jervis Tetch is obsessed with Lewis Carroll's famous book, *Alice's Adventures in Wonderland*. He believes himself to be the Mad Hatter, taking Carroll's crazy hatmaker's name as his own and donning a top hat. Tetch thinks a former coworker named Alice is the main character from Wonderland and that she is destined to marry him. This belief has led Tetch to create mind-control technology in order to brainwash Alice, and the rest of the world, into living out his crazy fantasy.

LEVEL: ★★☆

 1

Fold and unfold.

2
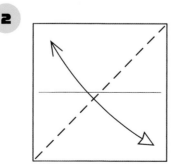
Fold and unfold.

3
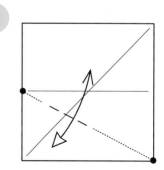
Fold and unfold by the diagonal.

4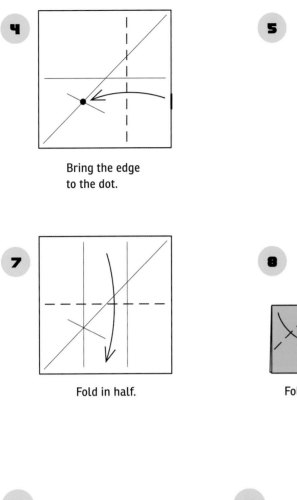

Bring the edge
to the dot.

5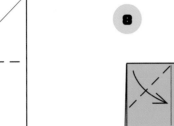

Fold to the right.

6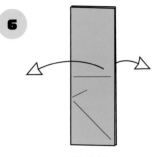

Unfold.

7

Fold in half.

8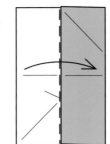

Fold to the creases.

9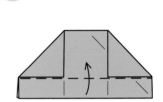

Fold the top layer
up. Repeat behind.

10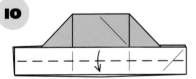

Fold down.
Repeat behind.

11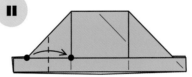

The dots will meet.

12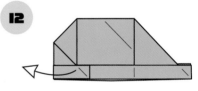

Unfold.

13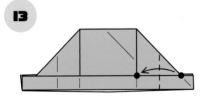

Repeat steps 11–12
on the right.

14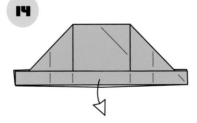

Unfold and repeat behind.

15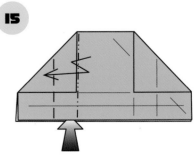

Crimp-fold along
the creases.

16

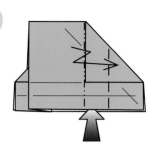

Crimp-fold along
the creases.

17

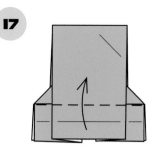

Fold up along the
crease. Repeat behind.

18

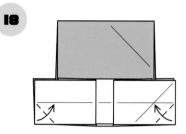

Fold all the layers
on the left and right.

19

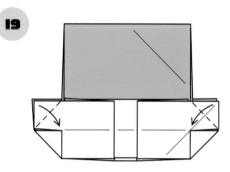

Fold the top layer on the left
and right. Repeat behind.

20

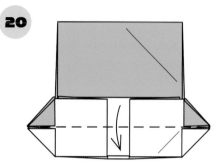

Fold down. Repeat behind.

21

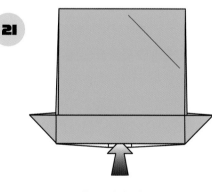

Round the hat
at the bottom.

22

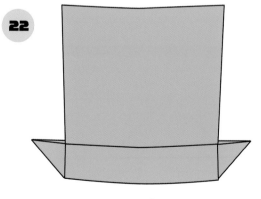

Mad Hatter's Top Hat

13

THE PENGUIN'S UMBRELLA

Oswald Cobblepot, known as the Penguin, is an emperor of Gotham City's business world—and its criminal underworld. Although often protected by hired goons, the Penguin does have a few rainy-day weapons hidden up his sleeve, including his infamous umbrella! This high-tech device can hide a variety of tools, including a machine gun, a flamethrower, or a blade. The umbrella can also double as a parachute or helicopter, allowing the super-villain to fly away from situations gone afowl.

LEVEL: ★★☆

I

Fold and unfold.

2

Fold to the center.

3

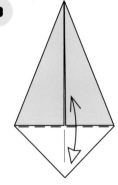

Fold and unfold.

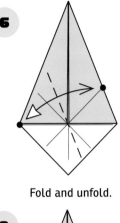

4

Fold and unfold.

5

Fold and unfold.

6

Fold and unfold.

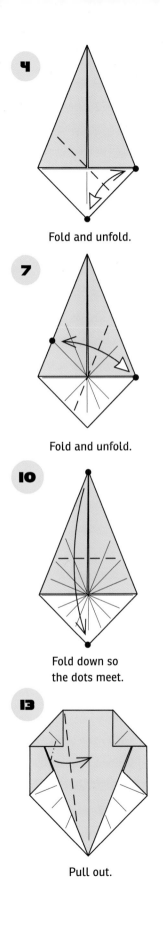

7

Fold and unfold.

8

Fold and unfold.

9

Fold and unfold.

10

Fold down so
the dots meet.

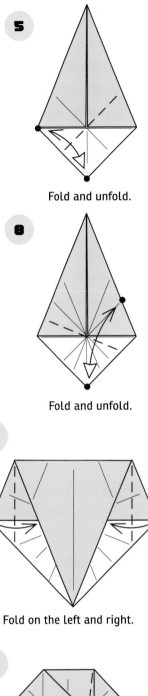

11

Fold on the left and right.

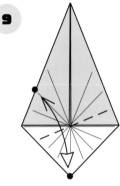

12

Fold at the dots.

13

Pull out.

14

Pull out and rotate
model 90°.

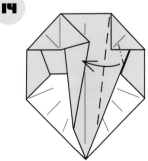

15

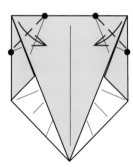

Fold down so the dots
meet and allow the
handle to swing
outward. Rotate model.

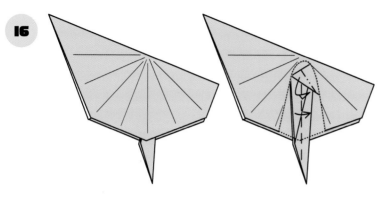

View of the inside. Thin the
handle, repeat behind.

Shape the handle
with reverse folds.

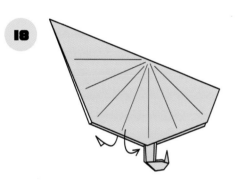

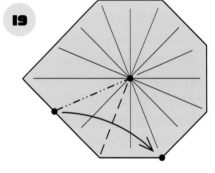

Spread the top.

View of the top. Puff out at
the dot in the center. The
other two dots will meet.

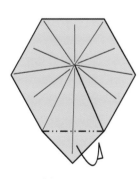

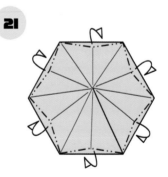

Wrap around.

Shape the rim.

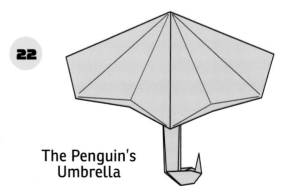

The Penguin's
Umbrella

BAT-SYMBOL

The bat-symbol strikes fear into the hearts of Gotham City's worst villains, but the symbol originated from Batman's greatest fear—bats! As a child, billionaire Bruce Wayne fell into a well that was swirling with a colony of terrifying bats. After the death of his parents, Bruce transformed this lifelong phobia into a new identity. He became Batman, the Caped Crusader. Although criminals now fear him, Batman and his symbol represent hope to the citizens of Gotham City.

LEVEL: ★★☆

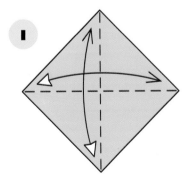

1

Fold and unfold.

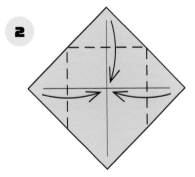

2

Fold three corners to the center.

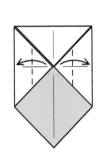

3

Fold the corners to the edges.

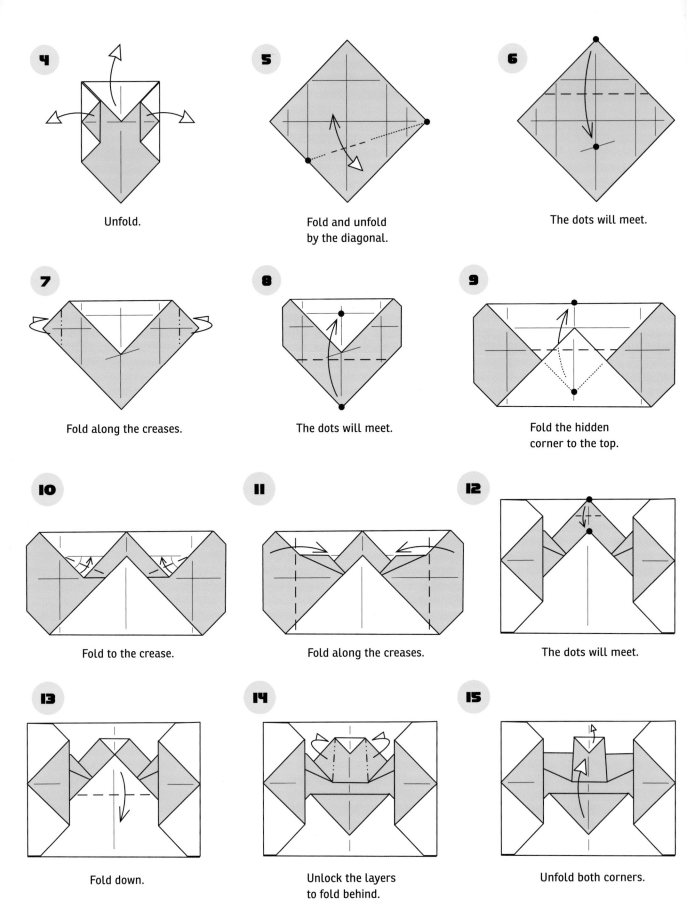

4 Unfold.

5 Fold and unfold by the diagonal.

6 The dots will meet.

7 Fold along the creases.

8 The dots will meet.

9 Fold the hidden corner to the top.

10 Fold to the crease.

11 Fold along the creases.

12 The dots will meet.

13 Fold down.

14 Unlock the layers to fold behind.

15 Unfold both corners.

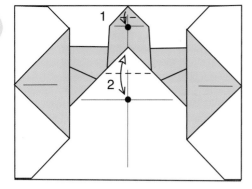

16

1. Fold down.
2. Fold and unfold.

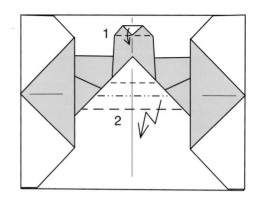

17

1. Fold down.
2. Pleat-fold. Valley-fold along the creases.

18

Fold behind.

19

Fold behind.

20

Fold behind.

21

Fold behind.

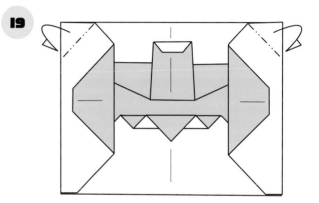

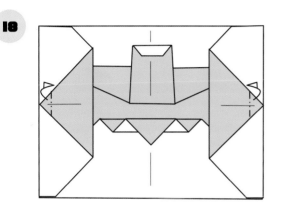

22

Bat-symbol

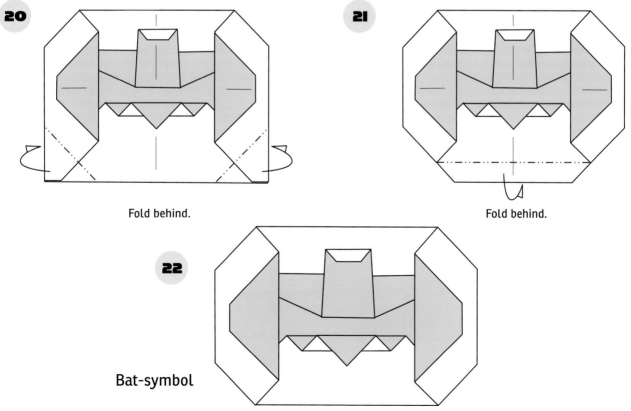

Batman takes on the world's worst criminals without using a gun. Instead, the Dark Knight equips himself with non-lethal gadgets, including his all-time favorite weapon, the Batarang! With the flick of Batman's wrist, this razor-sharp metal throwing device zings through the air at high speed. Although lightweight, a precisely thrown Batarang can take down any villain in Gotham City, even hulking brutes like Bane and Clayface.

LEVEL: ★★★

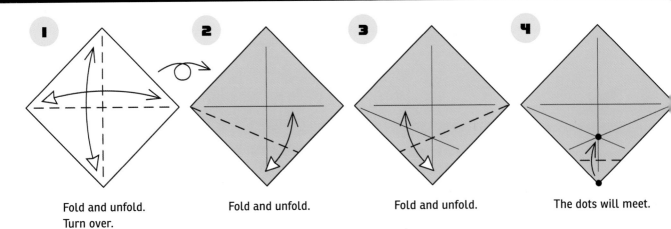

1 Fold and unfold. Turn over.

2 Fold and unfold.

3 Fold and unfold.

4 The dots will meet.

20

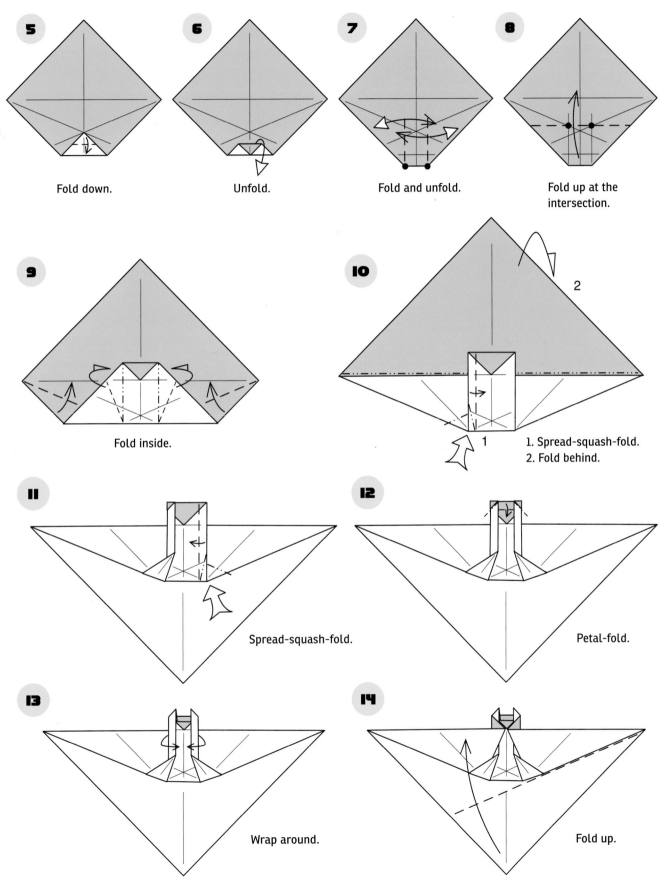

5 Fold down.

6 Unfold.

7 Fold and unfold.

8 Fold up at the intersection.

9 Fold inside.

10
1. Spread-squash-fold.
2. Fold behind.

11 Spread-squash-fold.

12 Petal-fold.

13 Wrap around.

14 Fold up.

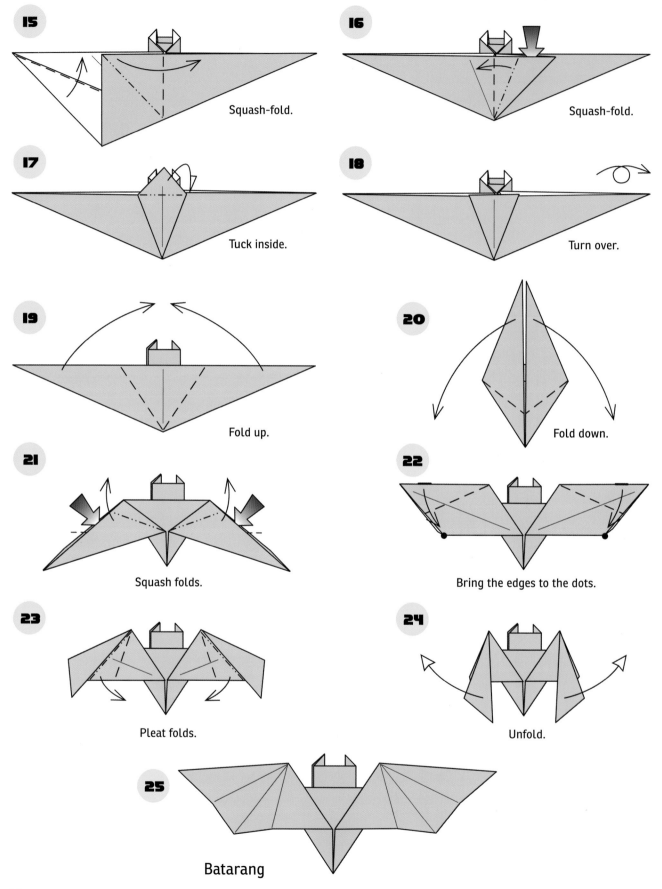

15 Squash-fold.

16 Squash-fold.

17 Tuck inside.

18 Turn over.

19 Fold up.

20 Fold down.

21 Squash folds.

22 Bring the edges to the dots.

23 Pleat folds.

24 Unfold.

25

Batarang

NIGHTWING SYMBOL

A seasoned pro at protecting the innocent, Nightwing once worked with the World's Greatest Detective, Batman. Now the fearless fighter flies solo. He graduated from his former role as Robin to become a stronger, sleeker creature of the night. Whether creating a fearsome threesome with the Dynamic Duo or surprising crooks on his own, Nightwing dons his blue emblem to dart from darkness when least expected.

LEVEL: ★★★

1

Fold and unfold.

2

Fold and unfold.

3

Fold to the center and unfold. Crease at the edge.

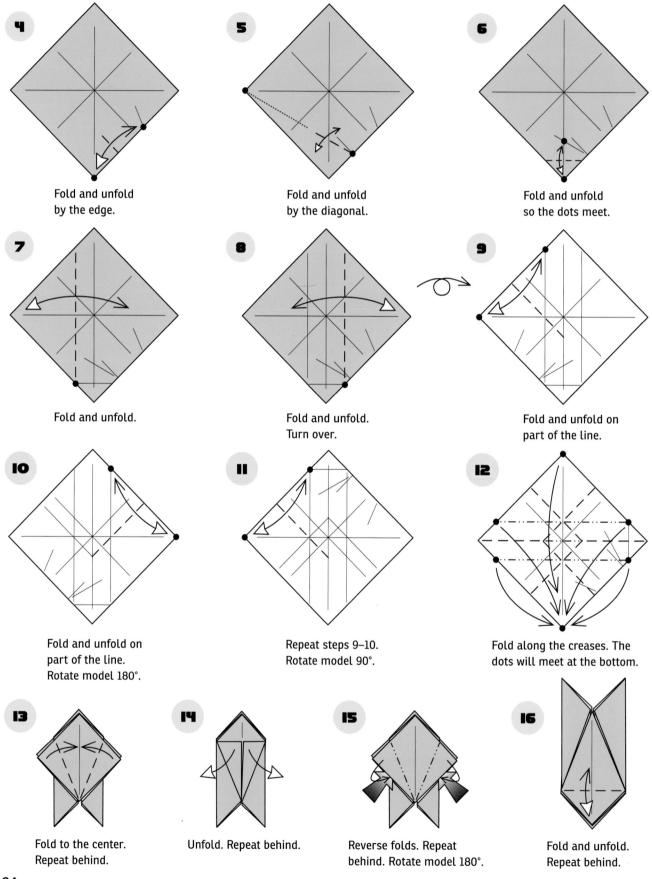

4 Fold and unfold by the edge.

5 Fold and unfold by the diagonal.

6 Fold and unfold so the dots meet.

7 Fold and unfold.

8 Fold and unfold. Turn over.

9 Fold and unfold on part of the line.

10 Fold and unfold on part of the line. Rotate model 180°.

11 Repeat steps 9–10. Rotate model 90°.

12 Fold along the creases. The dots will meet at the bottom.

13 Fold to the center. Repeat behind.

14 Unfold. Repeat behind.

15 Reverse folds. Repeat behind. Rotate model 180°.

16 Fold and unfold. Repeat behind.

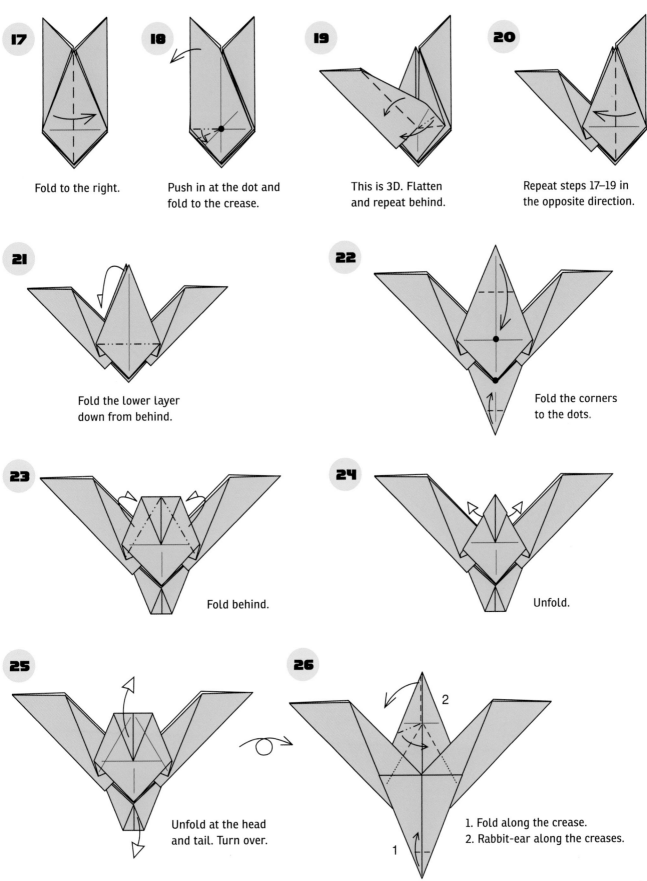

17 Fold to the right.

18 Push in at the dot and fold to the crease.

19 This is 3D. Flatten and repeat behind.

20 Repeat steps 17–19 in the opposite direction.

21 Fold the lower layer down from behind.

22 Fold the corners to the dots.

23 Fold behind.

24 Unfold.

25 Unfold at the head and tail. Turn over.

26
1. Fold along the crease.
2. Rabbit-ear along the creases.

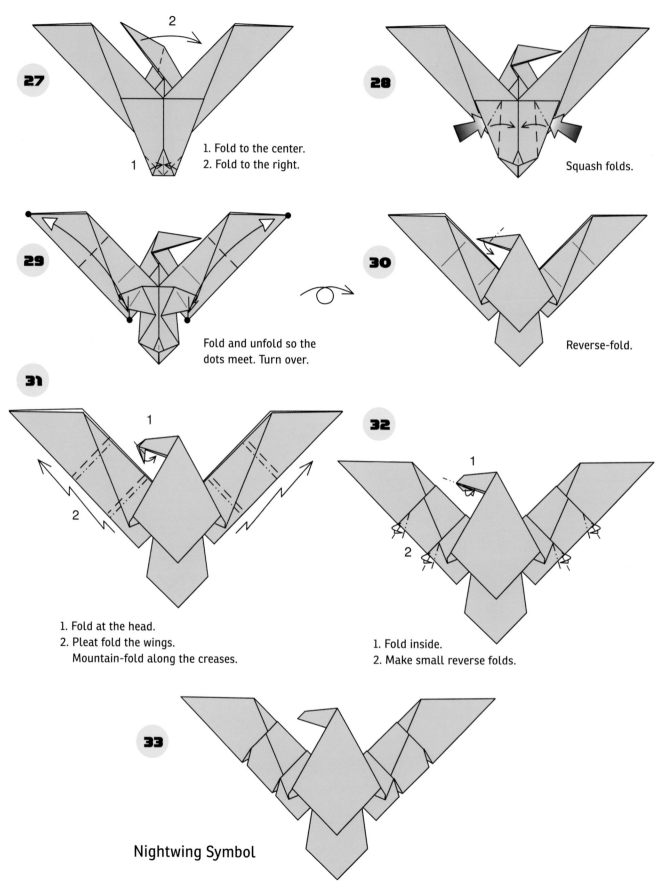

27
1. Fold to the center.
2. Fold to the right.

28
Squash folds.

29
Fold and unfold so the dots meet. Turn over.

30
Reverse-fold.

31
1. Fold at the head.
2. Pleat fold the wings.
   Mountain-fold along the creases.

32
1. Fold inside.
2. Make small reverse folds.

33

Nightwing Symbol

BATCYCLE

Batman's secret headquarters, the Batcave, is filled with dozens of high-tech vehicles, including the Batcycle. This quick, responsive motorcycle is the Dark Knight's preferred method of transportation on narrow and crowded roadways or when the Batmobile is under repair. Like the Batmobile, the Batcycle is a technological wonder. It sports a bulletproof wind-guard, computerized controls, and a 786 cc liquid-cooled V-4 engine.

LEVEL: ★★★

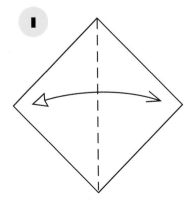

1

Fold and unfold.

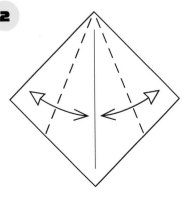

2

Fold to the center and unfold.

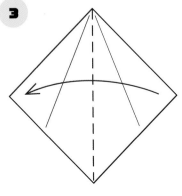

3

Fold in half.

27

4

Fold and unfold so the
dots meet. Rotate model.

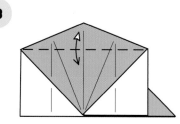

5

Squash-fold.

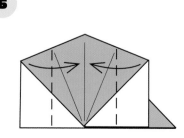

6

Fold to the center.

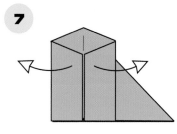

7

Unfold.

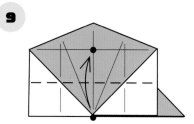

8

Fold and unfold.

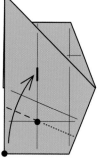

9

Fold up.

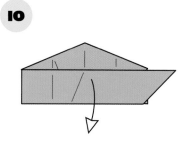

10

Unfold, turn over,
and rotate model.

11

Bring the corner to the
line. Crease on the left.

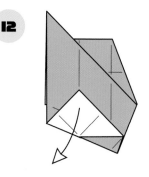

12

Unfold.

13

Bring the corner to the
line. Crease on the right.

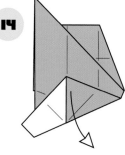

14

Unfold.

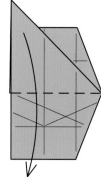

15

Fold down. Rotate
model 180°.

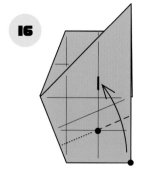

16

Repeat steps 11–14 in
the opposite direction.

28

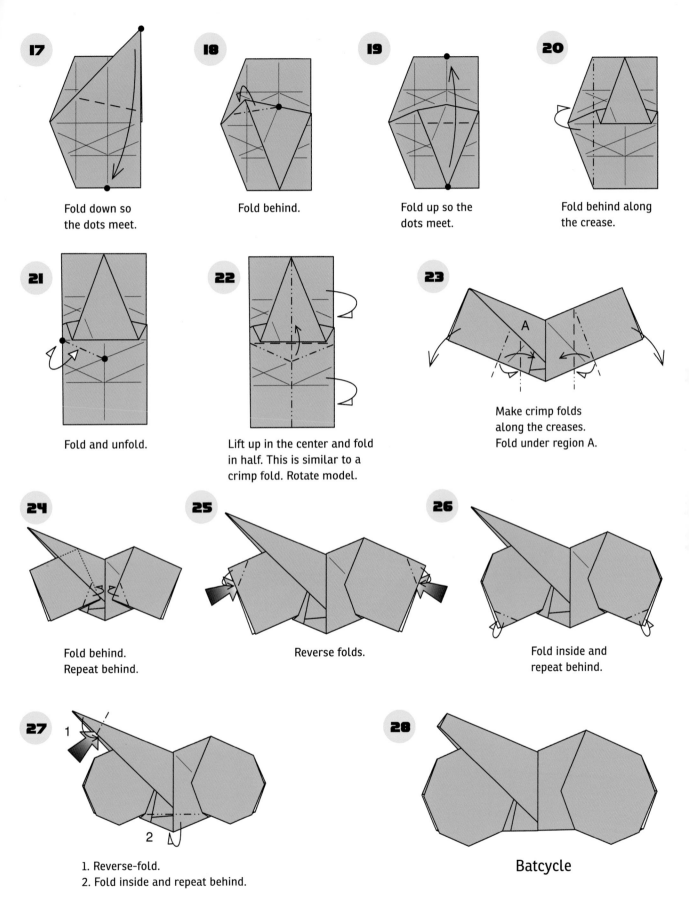

17 Fold down so the dots meet.

18 Fold behind.

19 Fold up so the dots meet.

20 Fold behind along the crease.

21 Fold and unfold.

22 Lift up in the center and fold in half. This is similar to a crimp fold. Rotate model.

23 Make crimp folds along the creases. Fold under region A.

24 Fold behind. Repeat behind.

25 Reverse folds.

26 Fold inside and repeat behind.

27
1. Reverse-fold.
2. Fold inside and repeat behind.

28 Batcycle

BATWING

When the Dark Knight needs a bat's-eye view of Gotham City, he lifts off in the Batwing. This high-tech aircraft rockets through the sky at supersonic speeds, but it is also capable of stealth takeoffs and landings. The Batwing includes many comforts of Batman's secret headquarters, the Batcave, such as a Batcomputer, a state-of-the-art communications system, and room for up to six passengers. The Dark Knight most often utilizes the Batwing for long-distance travel, air-to-air combat, and keeping up with his high-flying friends in the Justice League.

LEVEL: ★ ★ ★

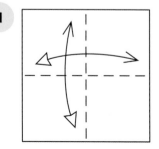

1

Fold and unfold.
Turn over.

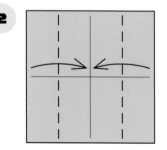

2

Fold to the center.

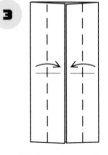

3

Fold to the center.

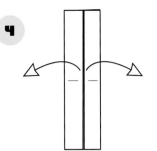

4

Unfold everything.

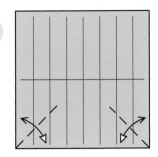

5

Fold and unfold at the bottom. Turn over.

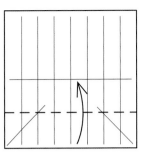

6

Fold to the crease.

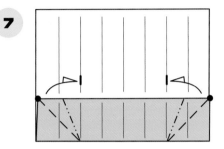

7

Fold inside so the dots meet the creases.

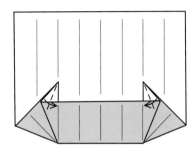

8

Fold the top layers.

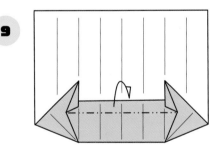

9

Fold inside.

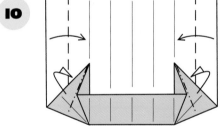

10

Reverse folds. Valley-fold along the creases.

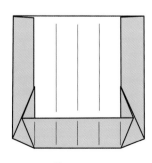

11

Turn over.

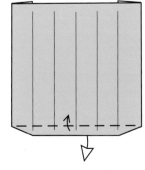

12

Fold up and swing out from behind.

13

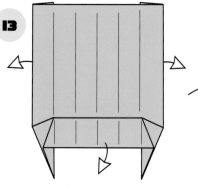

Unfold everything
and turn over.

14

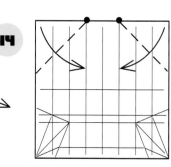

Fold to the creases.

15

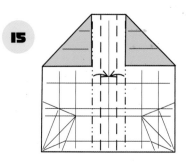

Pleat-fold. Mountain-fold
along the creases.

16

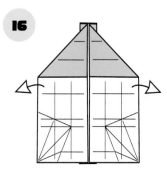

Unfold.

17

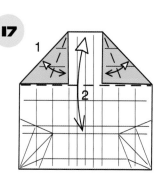

1. Fold and unfold both layers.
2. Fold and unfold.

18

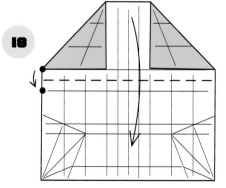

Fold down so
the dots meet.

19

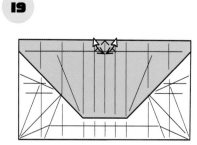

Fold and unfold.

20

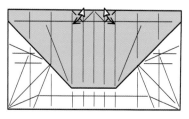

Fold and unfold.

21

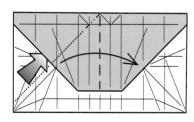

Squash-fold but only
crease at the top.

22

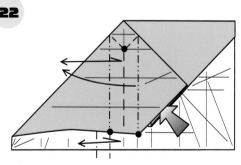

Push in at the upper dot. Bring
the two mountain fold lines
together, and pleat at the bottom.

23

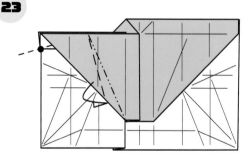

Fold inside. Begin with the
mountain fold along the crease
and continue to the dot.

24

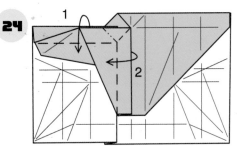

1. Fold down while ...
2. ... folding to the left.

25

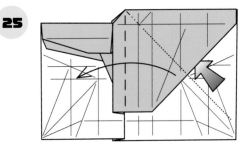

Repeat steps 21–24
on the right.

26

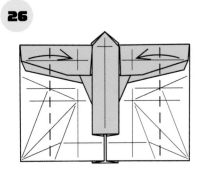

Fold along the creases.

27

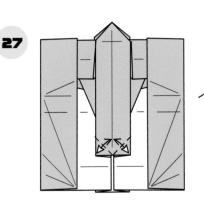

Fold and unfold.
Turn over.

28

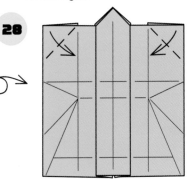

Fold to the creases.

29

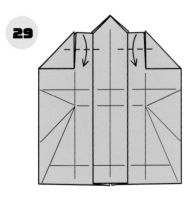

Fold down. Some of
the layers are hidden.

30

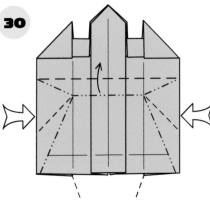

Fold along the creases.

31

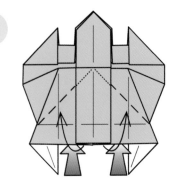

Lift at the bottom
and spread.

32

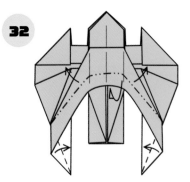

This is 3D. Fold inside along
the creases and flatten.

33

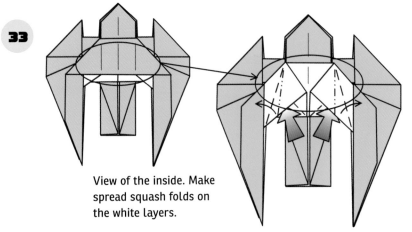

View of the inside. Make
spread squash folds on
the white layers.

34

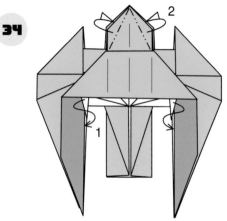

1. Tuck the white flaps under the darker paper.
2. Fold inside, repeat behind.

35

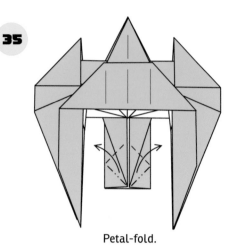

Petal-fold.

36

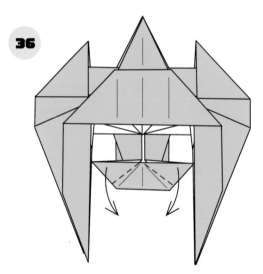

Fold down at an angle.

37

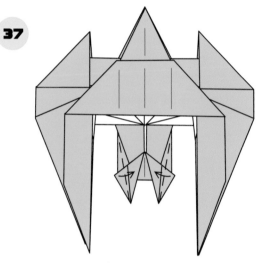

Thin the tips.

38

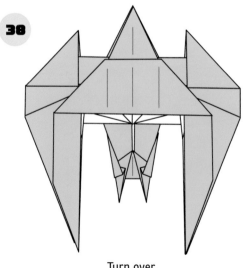

Turn over.

39

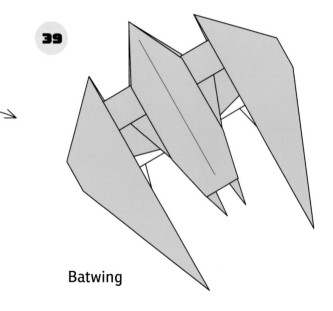

Batwing

CLAYFACE

Half-man, half-muck, Clayface is a monster with a human heart and brain. Formerly a famous film actor, Matt Hagen's face—and career—were ruined in a tragic car accident. Hoping to regain his good looks, Hagen accepted the help of Roland Daggett. The slimy businessman gave the actor a special cream that allowed him to reshape his face like clay. But Hagen became greedy and wanted more. Then he got caught stealing the ominous ointment. As punishment, the angry Daggett forced him to consume an entire barrel. But the supposedly deadly dose didn't kill Hagen. It turned him into a shape-shifting creature with only one thing on his muddy mind: revenge!

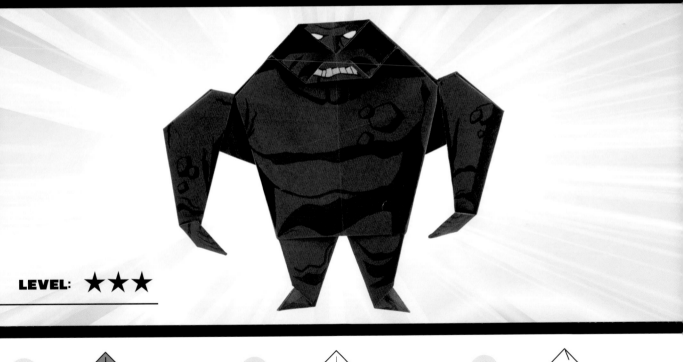

LEVEL: ★★★

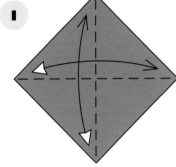

1

Fold and unfold.
Turn over.

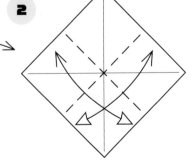

2

Fold and unfold.

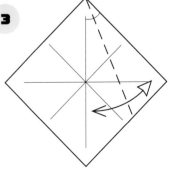

3

Fold and unfold
on the right.

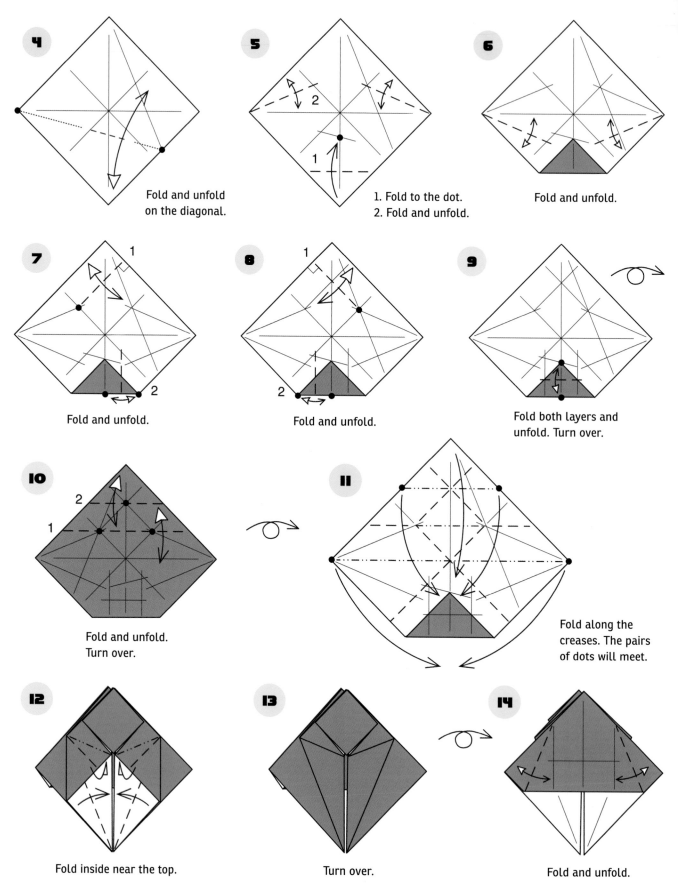

4 Fold and unfold on the diagonal.

5 1. Fold to the dot.
2. Fold and unfold.

6 Fold and unfold.

7 Fold and unfold.

8 Fold and unfold.

9 Fold both layers and unfold. Turn over.

10 Fold and unfold. Turn over.

11 Fold along the creases. The pairs of dots will meet.

12 Fold inside near the top.

13 Turn over.

14 Fold and unfold.

36

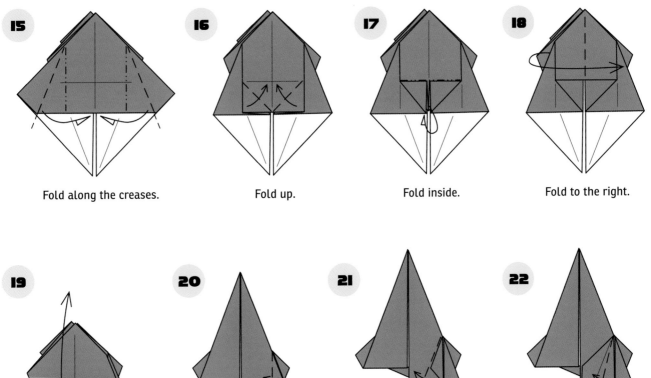

15 Fold along the creases.

16 Fold up.

17 Fold inside.

18 Fold to the right.

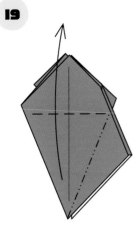 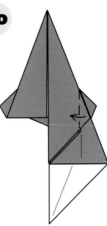

19 Squash-fold.

20 Fold to the left.

21 Fold to the left.

22 Fold to the left.

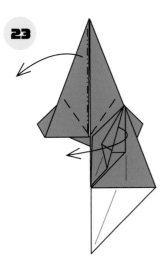 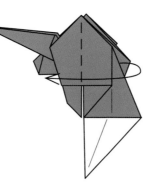 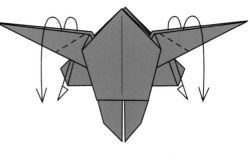

23 Fold to the left while folding the arm.

24 Repeat steps 18–23 on the right.

25 Outside-reverse folds.

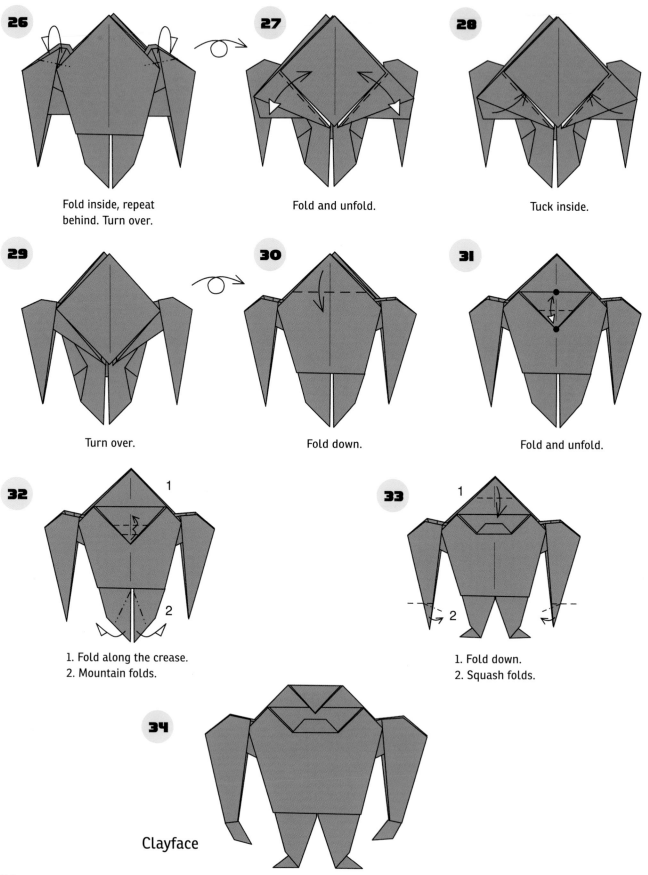

26 Fold inside, repeat behind. Turn over.

27 Fold and unfold.

28 Tuck inside.

29 Turn over.

30 Fold down.

31 Fold and unfold.

32
1. Fold along the crease.
2. Mountain folds.

33
1. Fold down.
2. Squash folds.

34 Clayface

Robin, the Boy Wonder, battles alongside Batman to rid Gotham City of evil and corruption. No hero can go it alone, and among crime fighters, Robin is the best wingman around. Once a member of a world-famous family of circus acrobats, Robin was orphaned as a child. He soon signed on with the Dark Knight, using his awesome athletic skills against big-time baddies. Robin's symbol reminds Gotham City's citizens that, like his namesake, he too can swoop down and snap up a crooked worm or two for the city jail!

LEVEL: ★★★

1

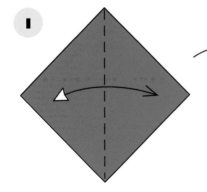

Fold and unfold.
Turn over.

2

Fold to the center.

3

Unfold and turn over.

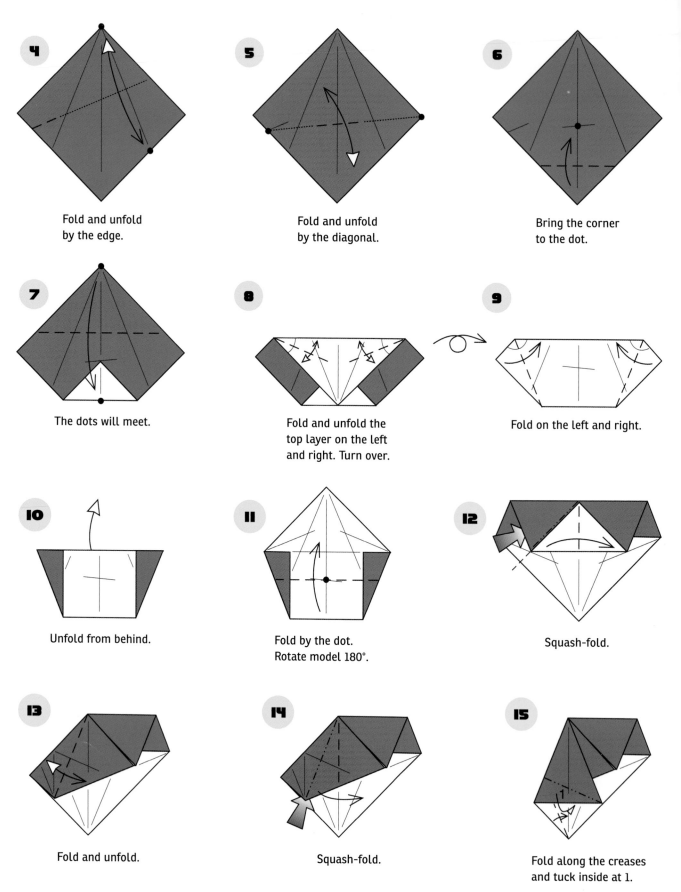

4 Fold and unfold by the edge.

5 Fold and unfold by the diagonal.

6 Bring the corner to the dot.

7 The dots will meet.

8 Fold and unfold the top layer on the left and right. Turn over.

9 Fold on the left and right.

10 Unfold from behind.

11 Fold by the dot. Rotate model 180°.

12 Squash-fold.

13 Fold and unfold.

14 Squash-fold.

15 Fold along the creases and tuck inside at 1.

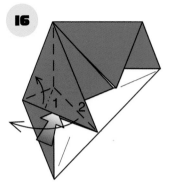

16

Lift up at 1 while folding to the left at 2.

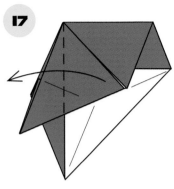

17

Fold to the left.

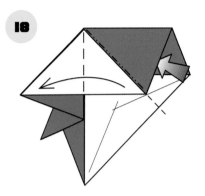

18

Repeat steps 12–17 on the right.

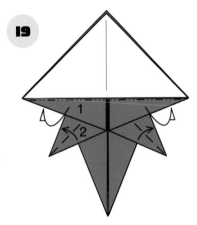

19

Fold behind at 1 while folding in half at 2.

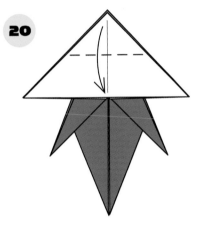

20

Fold down.

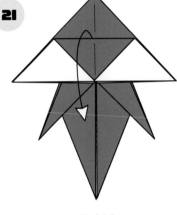

21

Unfold.

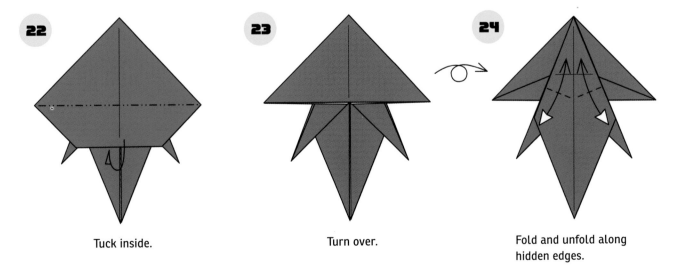

22

Tuck inside.

23

Turn over.

24

Fold and unfold along hidden edges.

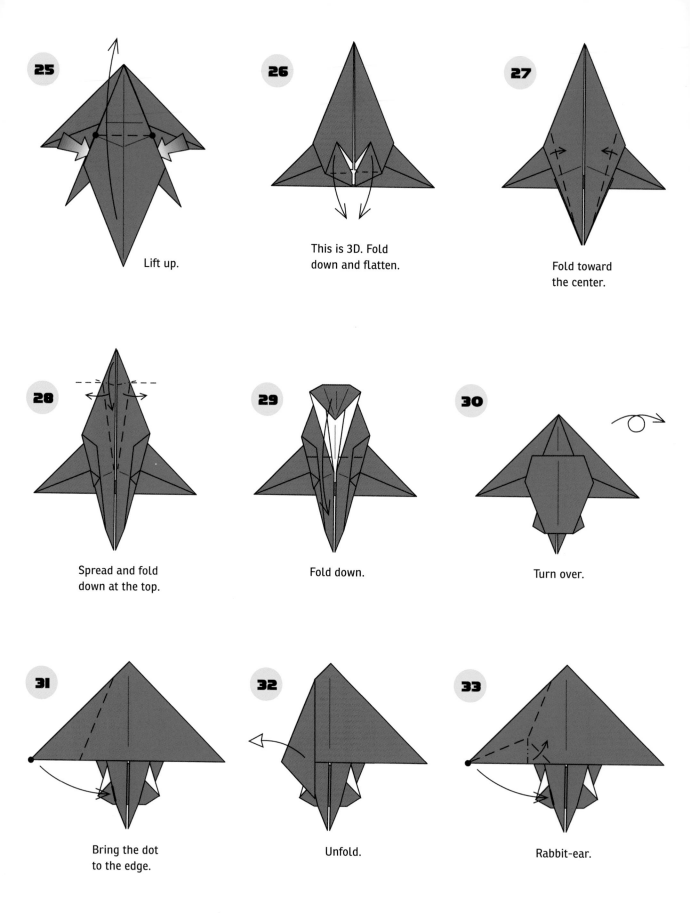

25

Lift up.

26

This is 3D. Fold
down and flatten.

27

Fold toward
the center.

28

Spread and fold
down at the top.

29

Fold down.

30

Turn over.

31

Bring the dot
to the edge.

32

Unfold.

33

Rabbit-ear.

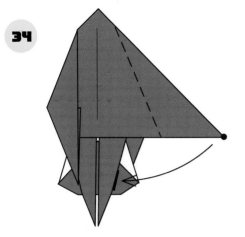

34

Repeat steps 31–33
on the right.

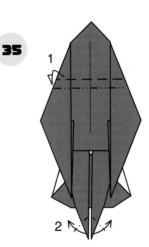

35

1. Pleat-fold between
   the body and cape.
2. Reverse-fold and
   spread the feet.

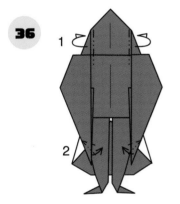

36

1. Fold behind and make
   small hidden squash folds
   at the neck.
2. Squash folds.

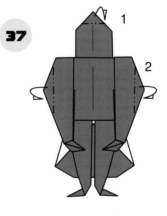

37

1. Fold behind.
2. Fold behind.

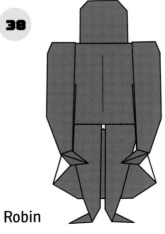

38

Robin

The world's worst criminals prowl Gotham City's streets, including the Joker, the Penguin, Catwoman, Poison Ivy, and Mr. Freeze. Thankfully, the city is protected by the World's Greatest Detective—Batman! While on a case, the Dark Knight protects himself with a flame-resistant cape, a high-tech cowl, and a Utility Belt filled with dozens of gadgets and weapons. Together, these items complete Batman's super hero uniform, known as the Batsuit.

LEVEL: ★★★

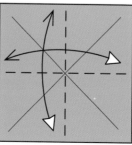

1

Fold and unfold.
Turn over.

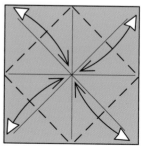

2

Fold and unfold.

3

Fold to the center and
unfold. Turn over.

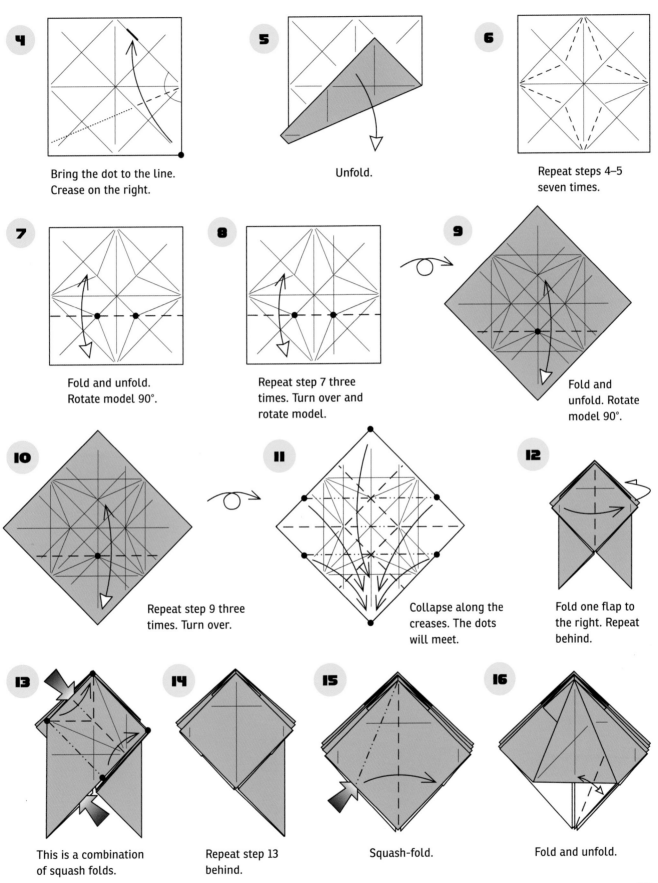

4

Bring the dot to the line.
Crease on the right.

5

Unfold.

6

Repeat steps 4–5
seven times.

7

Fold and unfold.
Rotate model 90°.

8

Repeat step 7 three
times. Turn over and
rotate model.

9

Fold and
unfold. Rotate
model 90°.

10

Repeat step 9 three
times. Turn over.

11

Collapse along the
creases. The dots
will meet.

12

Fold one flap to
the right. Repeat
behind.

13

This is a combination
of squash folds.

14

Repeat step 13
behind.

15

Squash-fold.

16

Fold and unfold.

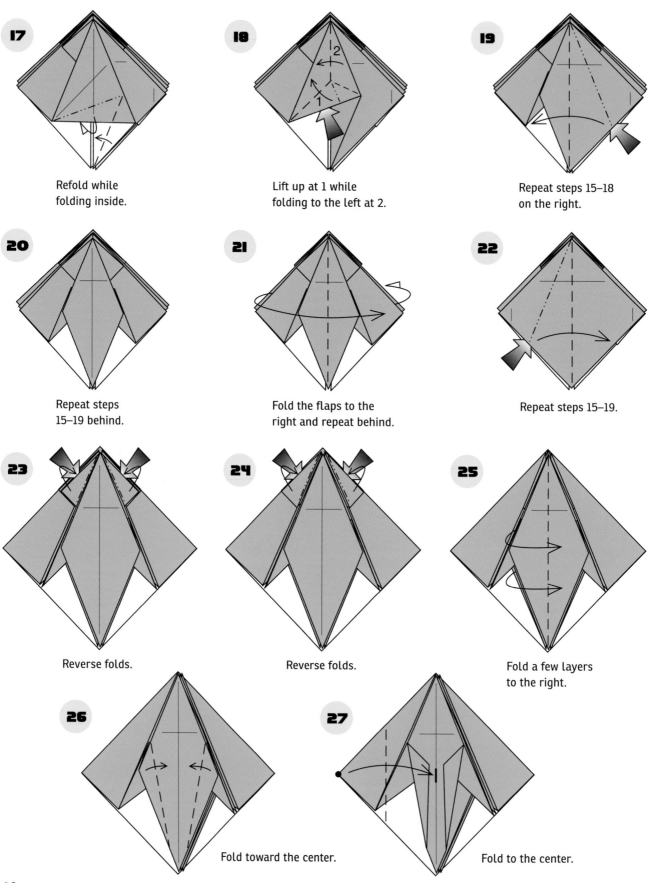

17 Refold while folding inside.

18 Lift up at 1 while folding to the left at 2.

19 Repeat steps 15–18 on the right.

20 Repeat steps 15–19 behind.

21 Fold the flaps to the right and repeat behind.

22 Repeat steps 15–19.

23 Reverse folds.

24 Reverse folds.

25 Fold a few layers to the right.

26 Fold toward the center.

27 Fold to the center.

28

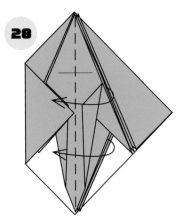

Fold a few layers
to the left.

29

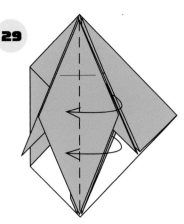

Repeat steps 25–28
on the right.

30

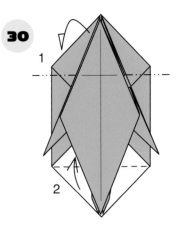

1. Fold behind.
2. Fold up.

31

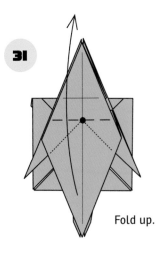

Fold up.

32

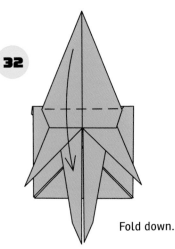

Fold down.

33

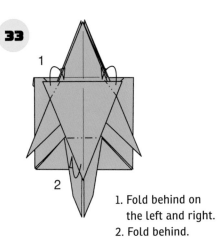

1. Fold behind on
   the left and right.
2. Fold behind.

34

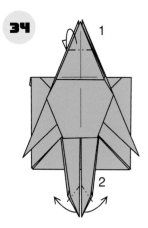

1. Fold behind.
2. Reverse folds.

35

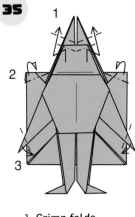

1. Crimp folds.
2. Fold behind.
3. Fold the hands.

36

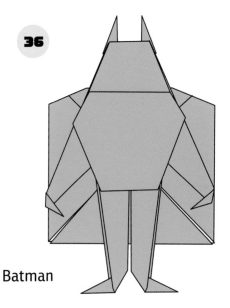

Batman

READ MORE

Harbo, Christopher. *Origami Palooza: Dragons, Turtles, Birds, and More!* Origami Paperpalooza. North Mankato, Minn.: Capstone Press, 2015.

Jackson, Paul. *Origami Zoo: 25 Fun Paper Animal Creations.* Layton, Utah: Gibbs Smith, 2011.

Montroll, John. *Dinosaur Origami.* New York: Dover Publications, 2010.

Montroll, John. *Justice League Origami: Amazing Folding Projects Featuring Green Lantern, Aquaman, and More.* DC Origami. North Mankato, Minn.: Capstone Press, 2015.

INTERNET SITES

FactHound offers a safe, fun way to find Internet sites related to this book. All of the sites on FactHound have been researched by our staff.

Here's all you do:

Visit *www.facthound.com*

Type in this code: 9781491417867

Super-cool stuff! Check out projects, games and lots more at **www.capstonekids.com**

ABOUT THE AUTHOR

John Montroll is respected for his work in origami throughout the world. His published work has significantly increased the global repertoire of original designs in origami. John is also acknowledged for developing new techniques and groundbreaking bases. The American origami master is known for being the inspiration behind the single-square, no cuts, no glue approach in origami.

John started folding in elementary school. He quickly progressed from folding models from books to creating his own designs. John has written many books, and each model that he designs has a meticulously developed folding sequence. John's long-standing experience allows him to accomplish a model in fewer steps rather than more. It is his constant endeavor to give the reader a pleasing folding experience.